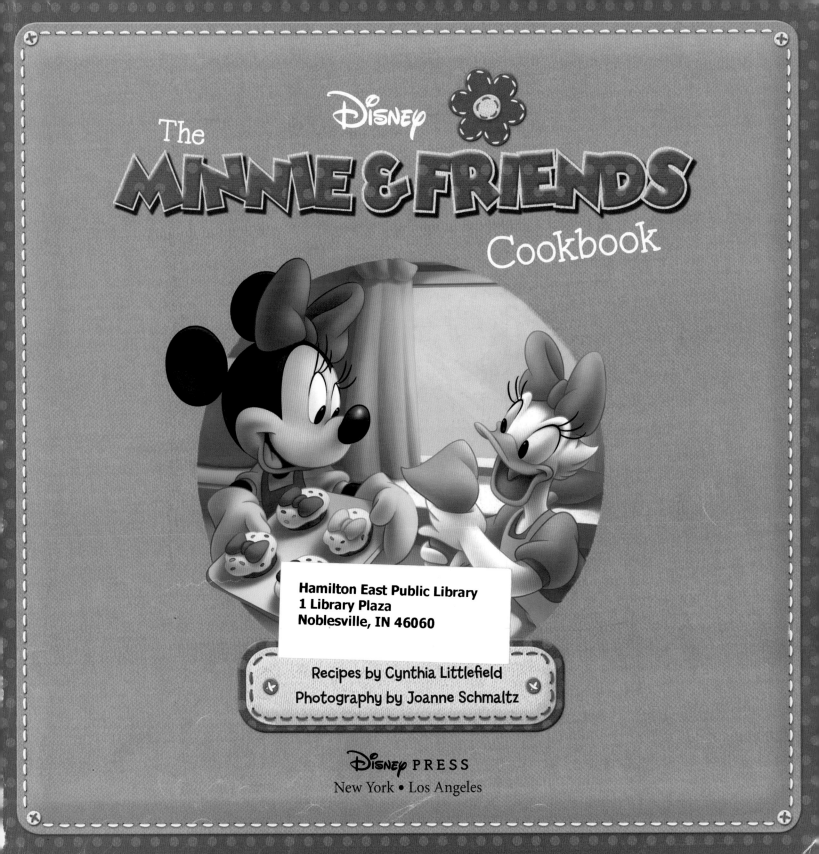

Disney

The MINNIE & FRIENDS Cookbook

Recipes by Cynthia Littlefield
Photography by Joanne Schmaltz

Disney PRESS
New York • Los Angeles

Dear Reader,

Did you know that when I was just a little mouse, I lived on a farm? That's where I learned to cook—helping turn the fruits and veggies we grew, the eggs we collected, and other fresh ingredients into delicious meals.

Now that I live in the city, I've spiced up those favorite family dishes to create recipes that are my very own. From the scrumptious muffins my nieces Millie and Melody love best, to my famous *Yoo-hoo!* Stew, to pretty pink mousse—you'll find them all here in this book!

I'm also including a few treats—like grilled cheese with a Goofy twist, Daisy's speedy stir-fry, and Mickey's tasty tacos—from friends who like to cook as much as I do.

I rated each recipe's difficulty on a five-bow scale: ⋈⋈⋈⋈⋈. That way, you'll know whether you're about to cook something easy (⋈) or complicated (⋈⋈⋈⋈⋈). So grab your apron and get ready to cook up some fantastic feasts!

Here are a few tips to keep in mind:

- ❁ Make sure you ask for a grown-up's permission *and* help before using a mixer, blender, stove, oven, or knife.

- ❁ Before you start cooking, tie your hair back and wear an apron. You don't want to end up with spots on your clothes—unless they're polka dots, of course. And be sure to wash your hands!

- ❁ Never touch a hot stove! Always use pot holders to move pans or baking sheets, both on the stove top and in and out of the oven.

- ❁ Remember, a good cook always leaves the kitchen spic-and-span. If you put everything back where it belongs, you'll know just where to find it next time.

Happy cooking!

Minnie Mouse

TABLE OF CONTENTS

BREAKFAST

Ear-resistible French Toast

Serves 2

There's no mistaking Minnie's signature French toast. Made with hints of cinnamon and vanilla, it looks a lot like her favorite mouse. No wonder it's the breakfast Mickey always flips over!

Ingredients

2 eggs

4 tablespoons milk

Dash of cinnamon

¼ teaspoon vanilla extract

6 slices whole wheat bread

Directions

1. Break the eggs into a shallow bowl.

2. Add the milk, cinnamon, and vanilla extract. Whisk the mixture until blended.

3. Use a medium-size (about 2¾ inches wide) round cookie cutter and a small (about 1½ inches wide) round cookie cutter to cut a head and two ear shapes from each slice of bread.

4. Lightly grease a nonstick frying pan. Warm the pan on the stove top over medium heat for one minute. Then turn the heat down to medium-low.

5. One at a time, dip the bread circles into the egg batter, coating both sides, and place them in the pan.

6. Cook the French toast circles until the bottoms are golden brown (about 1½ to 2 minutes). Then flip them over with a spatula, and brown the other sides.

7. For each serving, arrange a head and two ear shapes on a plate to look like Mickey Mouse. Top it with a little butter and maple syrup.

Daisy's Delicious Yogurt Parfaits

Makes 1

Here's a fun and stylish way to jump-start the day—spooning up a delicious fruit-topped parfait.

Ingredients

Small (6-ounce) container
  vanilla or lemon yogurt

Small (4.4-ounce) container
  fresh blueberries

4 tablespoons granola

Directions

1. Spoon half of the yogurt into the bottom of a parfait glass or sundae dish. Top it with all but one tablespoon of the granola.

2. Spoon the rest of the yogurt on top of the granola layer.

3. Sprinkle on the remaining granola, and garnish the parfait with a small handful of fresh blueberries.

Millie and Melody's Morning Muffins

Makes 1 dozen

Whenever Minnie's nieces, Millie and Melody, sleep over, she makes their favorite breakfast—a batch of these scrumptious sweet-and-spicy muffins.

Ingredients

1⅓ cups flour

1½ teaspoons baking soda

½ teaspoon cinnamon

¼ teaspoon salt

1 egg

1 mashed banana

⅓ cup canola oil

½ cup maple syrup

1 teaspoon vanilla extract

1 packed cup shredded carrot

1 Granny Smith apple, diced

⅓ cup raisins

⅓ cup finely chopped walnuts

Directions

1. Heat the oven to 350°F. Line a 12-cup muffin pan with baking cups.

2. In a small mixing bowl, whisk together the flour, baking soda, cinnamon, and salt.

3. In a large mixing bowl, whisk together the egg, mashed banana, canola oil, maple syrup, and vanilla extract.

4. Stir the flour mixture, shredded carrot, apple, raisins, and walnuts into the egg mixture just until the ingredients are evenly combined.

5. Spoon the batter into the muffin pan, dividing it equally among the cups.

6. Bake the muffins until a toothpick inserted into the middle comes out clean, about 20 to 22 minutes.

7. Let the muffins cool slightly on a wire rack before serving.

Minnie's Cheese and Veggie Scramble

Serves 2

Egg-cellent cooks like Minnie always whip up a good breakfast. Made with cheese and vegetable bits, this easy scramble is not only hearty—it tastes great!

Ingredients

4 large eggs

2 tablespoons milk

½ teaspoon salt

½ teaspoon ground pepper

1 tablespoon butter

4 tablespoons shredded cheddar cheese

¾ cup cooked broccoli bits

Directions

1. Crack the eggs into a small mixing bowl. Add the milk, salt, and ground pepper, and beat the ingredients together with a fork.

2. Melt the butter in a small skillet over medium-low heat, and then pour in the egg mixture.

3. Sprinkle the cheese and broccoli on top of the eggs.

4. Use a spatula to gently stir the eggs as they thicken and cook through, about 3 minutes.

5. Remove from the stove and serve.

Donald's Go Bananas! Pancakes

Makes 18

Everybody knows that Donald can be a little difficult at times, but it's easy to butter him up with a plateful of these fruit-filled mini pancakes.

Ingredients

1 cup flour

2 teaspoons baking powder

½ teaspoon salt

Dash of nutmeg

1 egg

1 cup milk

2 tablespoons canola oil

1 tablespoon maple syrup

1 banana

Directions

1. In a small mixing bowl, whisk together the flour, baking powder, salt, and nutmeg.

2. In a medium mixing bowl, whisk together the egg, milk, canola oil, and maple syrup.

3. Stir the flour mixture into the egg mixture with a wooden spoon, just until all the ingredients are mixed. The batter will be thin and lumpy, but don't stir too much—it will thicken on its own.

4. Cut the banana into ½-inch slices.

5. Lightly grease a large nonstick frying pan. Warm the pan over medium heat for one minute. Then turn the heat down to medium-low.

6. Spoon 1 tablespoon of batter onto the heated pan for each pancake, spacing them a couple of inches apart. Add a banana slice to the center of each one.

7. When the tops of the pancakes start to bubble and the bottoms are golden brown (about 1 to 1½ minutes), carefully flip them over with a spatula. Continue cooking the pancakes until the undersides are golden brown. Serve with butter and maple syrup.

LUNCH

Minnie's Polka-dot Tomato Soup	18
Sweet and Sassy Salad	20
Mickey Mouse Club Sandwich	22
Goofy's Grilled Cheese	24
Figaro's Crispy Fish Sticks	26

Serves 3–4

Leave it to Minnie to serve soup with style. This creamy tomato-and-corn blend, topped with melted cheese polka-dots, is one of her specialties.

Ingredients

2 slices of cheese (American or provolone)

1 (14.75-ounce) can creamed corn

1 (14.5-ounce) can diced fire-roasted tomatoes

1 tablespoon butter

Salt and pepper to taste

Directions

1. Use a small round cookie cutter to cut a bunch of circular "polka dots" from the sliced cheese. (If you don't have a small cookie cutter, any circular object with a raised edge will do. Even plastic bottle caps are perfect for this recipe!) Set the cheesy polka dots aside for now.

2. Combine the corn and diced tomatoes in a blender, and blend them until smooth.

3. Pour the mixture into a medium saucepan. Bring it to a slow simmer over medium-low heat.

4. Add the butter, salt, and pepper, and continue heating the soup, stirring all the while. Heat until the butter melts and blends evenly into the mixture.

5. Ladle the soup into serving bowls, and immediately top it with the cheese polka dots. Wait a minute or so for the cheese to soften and melt around the edges before serving.

Sweet and Sassy Salad

▶◀ ▶◀ Serves 2–3

Topped with homemade citrus dressing, this salad combines the fruits and vegetables Minnie and Daisy like best. It's the perfect lunch to share with best friends.

Ingredients

10-12 ounces leafy green lettuce

1 cup grated carrot

1 cucumber, sliced

Orange Ginger Dressing:

⅓ cup orange juice

2 teaspoons lemon juice

2 teaspoons canola oil

2 teaspoons honey

¼ cup fresh peas

sliced almonds

¼ cup fresh blueberries and/or raspberries

⅛ teaspoon ground ginger

⅛ teaspoon salt

Directions

1. Rinse the lettuce well with cold water and then pat the leaves dry with paper towels. Tear the lettuce into bite-size pieces, and put some on each salad plate.

2. Top the lettuce with some grated carrot, several cucumber slices, and a spoonful of fresh peas. Add several berries and a sprinkling of sliced almonds.

3. In a small bowl, whisk together the citrus dressing ingredients. Spoon dressing onto each salad, and serve.

Mickey Mouse Club Sandwich

Serves 2

There's nothing Mickey likes to eat more for lunch than sandwiches. Stuffed with turkey, bacon, and fresh veggies, this double-decker sure fits the bill.

Ingredients

2 tablespoons mayonnaise

¼ teaspoon onion powder

¼ teaspoon celery salt

3 slices of whole wheat bread

2 lettuce leaves

3 turkey slices

3 tomato slices

3 strips of cooked bacon

Directions

1. In a small bowl, stir together the mayonnaise, onion powder, and celery salt.

2. Toast the bread. Spread a light coating of the seasoned mayonnaise on one of the slices. Then top it with a lettuce leaf and the turkey slices.

3. Set the second slice of toast on top, and press down lightly. Spread a little more mayonnaise on top of the toast and then layer the tomato slices, bacon, and second lettuce leaf.

4. Spread mayonnaise on the third toast slice, and place it (coated side down) on top of the sandwich. Press down lightly to stick the sandwich fillings together.

5. Cut the sandwich into four triangles, and poke a toothpick down through the center of each triangle. Place two of the triangles on each serving plate.

Goofy's Grilled Cheese

▶◀▶◀▶◀ Makes 1

Goofy has a knack for making amazing, if accidental, discoveries—like this wacky grilled cheese with crunchy pickle slices tucked into the middle.

Ingredients

½ tablespoon butter, softened

2 slices of whole wheat bread

2 slices of cheese (American, cheddar, or provolone)

Dill or bread-and-butter pickles, sliced

Directions

1. Spread butter on one side of each bread slice. Flip over one slice so that the buttered side faces down, and top it with a slice of cheese.

2. Use a piece of paper towel to pat the pickles dry and then layer them on the sandwich. Top the pickles with the remaining cheese slice and the second bread slice, this time buttered side up.

3. Heat a small nonstick frying pan over medium heat for 1 minute. Turn the heat down to low, and place the sandwich in the pan. Cover the pan, and grill the sandwich for 2½ minutes.

4. Use a spatula to flip the sandwich and gently but firmly press down on the top. Re-cover the pan, and continue grilling the sandwich until the cheese is melted and the flip side is browned (another 2 to 3 minutes).

5. Transfer the grilled sandwich to a plate, slice it in half, and serve.

Figaro's Crispy Fish Sticks

Serves 2–3

Coated with extra-flaky bread crumbs, these homemade codfish sticks are the cat's meow.

Ingredients

¼ cup flour

¼ teaspoon paprika

¼ teaspoon salt

⅛ teaspoon ground pepper

1 egg

⅔ cup panko bread crumbs

1 tablespoon grated Parmesan cheese

½ pound fresh cod loin

Directions

1. Heat the oven to 400°F. Grease a baking sheet.

2. In a small bowl, whisk together the flour, paprika, salt, and ground pepper.

3. Break the egg into a second bowl, and beat it with a fork.

4. In a third bowl, stir together the panko bread crumbs and grated Parmesan cheese.

5. Cut the cod loin into eight rectangular pieces that are roughly the same size.

6. One at a time, roll each piece of fish in the flour mixture and then dip it in the beaten egg. Next roll each fish stick in the bread crumb mixture, and place it on the baking sheet.

7. Bake the fish sticks for 10 minutes. Remove the pan from the oven and use a spatula or tongs to turn the fish sticks over. Then bake them for another 8 to 10 minutes. When done, the bread crumbs should be lightly browned and the fish should flake apart easily when pressed with a fork.

8. Serve with ketchup or tartar sauce.

DINNER

Oh, Boy! Tacos

Makes 8

Everyone loves the secret spice blend in Mickey's famous tacos. Whenever his friends hear that tacos are on the menu, they cheer Mickey's signature phrase: *Oh, boy!*

Ingredients

1 tablespoon cornstarch

1 tablespoon onion powder

1 tablespoon chili powder

2 tablespoons garlic powder

2 teaspoons cumin

2 teaspoons paprika

½ teaspoon salt

1 pound ground beef

1 cup water

8 taco shells

Optional Toppings:

Diced fresh tomatoes

Shredded lettuce

Shredded cheddar cheese

Sour cream

Directions

1. In a small bowl, stir together the cornstarch, onion powder, chili powder, garlic powder, cumin, paprika, and salt until evenly blended.

2. Brown the ground beef in a frying pan over medium-low heat. Drain any excess fat from the pan.

3. Add the water and spice blend to the pan, and stir until the beef is evenly coated. Cook the mixture over low heat, stirring occasionally, until it is thick and saucy.

4. Serve the seasoned beef and the remaining ingredients buffet-style so that everyone can fill their own tacos.

Minnie's Magnificent Meatballs

Makes about 1 dozen

Mamma mia, Minnie's on a roll with these amazing meatballs! Baked in the oven and then simmered in sauce, you can serve them with pasta or topped with cheese on a grinder roll.

Ingredients

1 large (32-ounce) jar tomato sauce

1 pound ground beef (85 percent lean)

1 egg

½ cup seasoned bread crumbs

¼ cup grated Parmesan cheese

1 teaspoon crushed dried oregano

½ teaspoon garlic powder

¼ teaspoon salt

⅛ teaspoon pepper

Directions

1. Heat oven to 425°F. Lightly grease a baking sheet.

2. Measure ½ cup of tomato sauce from the jar into a large mixing bowl, and pour the rest into a large saucepan. Set the saucepan aside.

3. Add the other ingredients to the mixing bowl, and mix everything together (with a wooden spoon or by hand) until well blended. Shape the mixture into 1½-inch meatballs.

4. Arrange the meatballs on the baking sheet, and bake them for 8 minutes. Remove the tray from the oven, and use a spatula or tongs to turn the meatballs over. Continue baking them until the outsides brown and they are cooked through (about 6 to 8 minutes).

5. Add the meatballs to the pan of sauce. Cover the pan, and bring the sauce to a simmer over medium heat. Lower the heat, and continue simmering for 20 minutes, stirring occasionally.

6. Serve with pasta, or use bread to create a meatball sandwich.

Daisy's Speedy Stir-Fry

Serves 4–6

Dinners by Daisy always cause a stir, especially when this beef-and-broccoli medley is on the menu.

Ingredients

2/3 cup cold water

2 tablespoons cornstarch

⅓ cup reduced sodium soy sauce

1 tablespoon brown sugar

1 teaspoon ground ginger

½ teaspoon garlic powder

2 tablespoons canola oil

¾ pound sirloin tips, sliced into thin bite-size pieces

3 cups broccoli florets

Directions

1. Pour the water into a small mixing bowl, and stir in the cornstarch until it is completely dissolved. Add the soy sauce, brown sugar, ground ginger, and garlic powder. Stir until well blended.

2. Place the canola oil and sliced steak in a large nonstick skillet, and stir-fry over medium-high heat until cooked through (about 5 minutes).

3. Remove the sirloin tips from the pan with a slotted spoon and set aside in a small bowl. Add the broccoli to the skillet and stir-fry for 2 minutes. Then, return the sirloin tips to the skillet.

4. Pour the soy sauce mixture over the broccoli and steak, and stir to evenly coat all the pieces. Bring the sauce to a simmer, and continue cooking and stirring just until the liquid starts to thicken.

5. Serve the stir-fry with a helping of brown rice or couscous.

Yoo-hoo! Stew

Serves 6

This saucy chicken-and-potato stew never fails to be a big hit with Minnie and her crew.

Ingredients

3¼ cups water, divided

1 teaspoon salt

2 medium-size red potatoes, scrubbed and diced (about 2 cups)

1 cup frozen corn

1 cup frozen peas

4 cups chicken broth

Whole cooked chicken breast, shredded or chopped into bite-size pieces

¼ teaspoon poultry seasoning

3 tablespoons cornstarch

1 cup mashed potato flakes

Salt and pepper to taste

Directions

1. Combine 3 cups of water, salt, and diced potatoes in a large pot. Bring the water to a low boil, and cook the potatoes until they are just tender enough to break with a fork, about 5 to 7 minutes.

2. Combine the corn and peas in a small colander or strainer and run cold water over them for a minute or so until thawed.

3. Stir the thawed vegetables, chicken broth, shredded chicken, and poultry seasoning into the pot of potatoes and cooking water.

4. Bring the mixture to a boil. Then lower the heat and simmer the stew for 3 or 4 minutes.

5. Pour the remaining ¼ cup of water into a small bowl, and stir in the cornstarch. Pour the dissolved cornstarch into the stew, stirring continuously. Simmer the stew for another 1 or 2 minutes to thicken it.

6. Stir in mashed potato flakes. Season the stew with salt and pepper, and serve.

Easy Pea-sy Bow Ties and Cheese

Serves 4

Featuring polka-dot peas and bow tie pasta, Minnie's mac-and-cheese is fancy *and* flavorful.

Ingredients

3 cups uncooked whole wheat
  bow tie pasta (farfalle)

3 tablespoons butter

2 tablespoons flour

½ cup chicken broth

1 cup low-fat milk

½ cup shredded or grated
  Parmesan cheese

1 teaspoon onion powder

¼ teaspoon garlic powder

¼ teaspoon salt

Dash of nutmeg

1 cup frozen peas

Directions

1. Bring a pot of water to a boil. Stir in pasta and let it cook, setting a timer for 8 minutes.

2. Meanwhile, melt the butter in a small saucepan over medium-low heat. Add the flour and chicken broth, and whisk until the flour dissolves.

3. Stir in the milk, Parmesan cheese, onion powder, garlic powder, salt, and nutmeg. Continue to heat and stir the mixture until the sauce thickens.

4. When the pasta timer goes off, add the frozen peas to the pot of cooking pasta. Cook the pasta for another minute or so, until it is done but still firm.

5. Strain the pasta and peas in a colander and then transfer them to a large bowl. Pour on the sauce. Stir until the pasta is evenly coated, and serve.

Polka-dot Pizza

Serves 3-4

Call it pizza with pizzazz. This festive pie is all decked out with diced "confetti" peppers and fresh mozzarella polka dots.

Ingredients

1 tablespoon cornmeal

1 (16-ounce) batch of pre-made pizza dough

Flour

¾ cup tomato sauce

½ cup grated Parmesan cheese

1 cup diced red and/or green bell pepper

½ to 1 cup diced ham (optional)

1 tablespoon olive oil

1 cup mini mozzarella balls (pearls)

Directions

1. Heat the oven to 400°F. Lightly grease a round pizza pan or rectangular baking sheet and then sprinkle the cornmeal over it.

2. Place the pizza dough on a flour-dusted surface. Use a rolling pin to roll out the dough to fit the pan you're using. Then transfer it to the prepared baking sheet.

3. Spread the tomato sauce on the dough, leaving a thin band around the outer edge uncovered. Sprinkle on the grated Parmesan, diced pepper, and diced ham (if you're including it). Drizzle on the olive oil.

4. Bake the pizza until the bottom crust is evenly browned, about 18 to 20 minutes. To check it, carefully lift a portion of the edge with a spatula.

5. Arrange the mini mozzarella balls on top of the pizza and then return it to the oven for another 2 to 3 minutes to melt the fresh cheese.

6. Slice and serve.

BREADS, SIDES, & DRINKS

Ribbon Swirl Salad

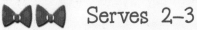 Serves 2–3

Being the fashionable mouse that she is, Minnie is a pro at tying bows. But that's not all—she can even weave veggie ribbons into a stylish side.

Ingredients

1 seedless cucumber, scrubbed

Bowl of ice water

1 medium carrot, scrubbed and peeled

1 tablespoon of your favorite salad dressing

Directions

1. Slice the ends off the cucumber and discard them. Then cut the cucumber into 8-inch sections. Use a vegetable peeler to slice ribbons from each section, and put them into the bowl of ice water.

2. Prepare the carrot as you did the cucumber, adding the ribbons to the bowl.

3. Let the ribbons soak in the water for 15 to 20 minutes to crisp them up. Then, drain them in a colander. Dry the bowl, and put the ribbons back in it. Drizzle on the salad dressing, toss, and serve.

Pluto's Baked Hush Puppies

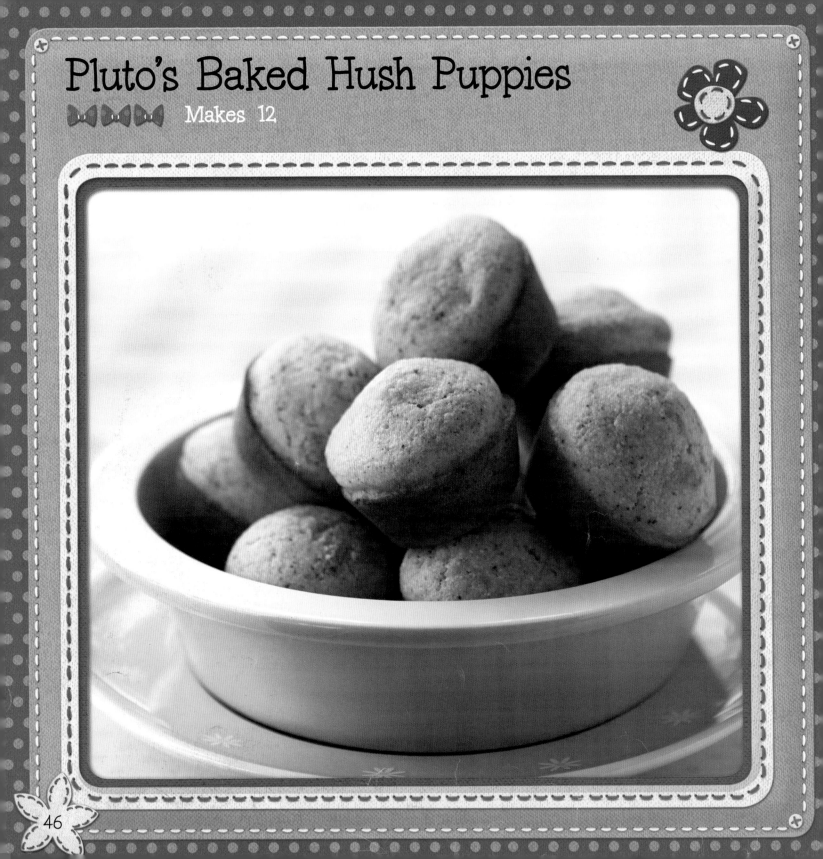

Just ask Mickey's faithful pup: these savory cornbread balls are doggone delicious!

Ingredients

½ cup cornmeal

¼ cup flour

1 teaspoon baking powder

¾ teaspoon onion powder

½ teaspoon chili powder

¼ teaspoon salt

1 egg

¼ cup milk

3 tablespoons canola oil

1 tablespoon honey

Directions

1. Heat the oven to 425°F. Grease a 12-cup mini muffin pan.

2. In a small mixing bowl, whisk together the cornmeal, flour, baking powder, onion powder, chili powder, and salt.

3. In a medium mixing bowl, whisk together the egg, milk, canola oil, and honey.

4. Stir the flour mixture into the egg mixture, just until the batter is evenly blended.

5. Spoon the batter into the muffin pan, dividing it equally among the cups. Bake the hush puppies until a toothpick inserted into the middle comes out clean (about 6 to 8 minutes), and serve while warm.

PLUTO

Minnie's Lemon Carrots

▶◀ ▶◀ ▶◀ Serves 3–4

As a talented gardener, Minnie has a real knack for preparing veggies in super-yummy ways—like adding a lemony zip to cooked carrots!

Ingredients

3 large carrots

⅓ cup water

1 tablespoon butter

1 tablespoon honey

1 teaspoon fresh lemon juice

Dash of salt

Directions

1. Scrub and peel the carrots. Cut off and discard the tops and tips. Then cut the carrots into ¼-inch slices.

2. Combine the carrot slices, water, butter, and honey in a medium-size frying pan. Bring the mixture to a boil. Then turn the heat down just enough to cook the carrots at a low boil, stirring occasionally to evenly distribute the butter and honey.

3. When most of the water has evaporated and the carrots are just tender enough to poke a fork through, stir in the lemon juice and salt.

4. Turn the heat down to low, and cook the carrots for another minute or so before serving.

Daisy's Jitterbug Juice

🎀 Serves 2

A dazzling dancer like Daisy can really work up a thirst. When it comes to refreshments, this fizzy fruit drink is her top choice.

Ingredients

1 cup unsweetened pineapple juice
½ cup lemonade
1 cup seltzer water

Ice
2 lemon slices

Directions

1. Stir the pineapple juice and lemonade together in a pitcher or quart-size measuring cup.

2. Slowly pour in the seltzer water.

3. Pour the juice mixture into tall glasses filled with ice. Add a lemon slice to each glass, and serve.

Mickey's Moo-shake

Makes 1

Mickey and Minnie love to make these frothy purple shakes whenever they have a moo-vie night.

Ingredients

½ cup unsweetened purple grape juice

1 banana, peeled and sliced

Vanilla frozen yogurt or ice cream

Low-fat milk

Directions

1. Combine the grape juice and sliced banana in a blender.

2. Put a small scoop of the frozen yogurt or ice cream into a 1-cup measuring cup. Now pour in enough low-fat milk to fill the cup. Add the contents of the cup to the juice and banana.

3. Blend the ingredients until the shake is smooth and frothy, about 1 minute, and then pour it into a tall glass. If you like, top the moo-shake with a small spoonful of frozen yogurt or ice cream, and enjoy!

DESSERT

Mouse-tacular Chocolate Cookies	54
Huey, Dewey, & Louie Triple-Fruit Crisp	56
Minnie Mouse Mousse	58
Daisy's Daisy Cupcake Decorations	60
Polka-dot Fruit Sundae	62

Mouse-tacular Chocolate Cookies

Makes 1½ dozen

What do you get when a dynamic duo like Minnie and Mickey put their heads together? A batch of double-icious chocolaty cookies.

Ingredients

¼ cup powdered sugar

¾ cup flour

⅓ cup cocoa powder

¾ teaspoon baking powder

⅛ teaspoon salt

¼ cup butter, softened

¾ cup sugar

1 egg

¼ teaspoon vanilla extract

½ cup chocolate chips

Nonpareil candies or similar-shaped chocolate drops

Mini bow-shape cake-decorating candies

Directions

1. Heat the oven to 350°F. Line two baking sheets with parchment paper. Measure the powdered sugar into a small bowl and set it aside.

2. In a small mixing bowl, whisk together the flour, cocoa powder, baking powder, and salt.

3. Combine the softened butter and sugar in a large mixing bowl, and beat them with an electric mixer until light and creamy. Next, beat in the egg and vanilla extract.

4. Add the flour mixture one half at a time, beating after each addition.

5. Roll a spoonful of the batter into a 1¼-inch ball. Roll the bottom of the ball in the powdered sugar and place it (coated side down) on one of the prepared baking sheets. Repeat this step, spacing the dough balls a couple of inches apart.

6. Bake the cookies until they puff up and the tops crack, about 8 to 10 minutes. (Don't overbake them!) Set the baking sheets atop cooling racks, leaving the cookies on them until they've cooled.

7. Heat the chocolate chips in a microwavable bowl for one minute with the microwave set at 50 percent power. Stir the chips and then heat them for another 15 seconds. Stir again. Continue doing this until the chips blend together.

8. Use the tip of a spoon to flatten two spots at the top edge of each cookie for attaching candy "ears." For each ear, dip the lower portion of a nonpareil candy into the melted chocolate. Gently but firmly press the ear in place (with the white candy-coated side facing down).

9. Dip part of a mini bow-shaped candy, and stick it to the base of the ears on half of the cookies.

Huey, Dewey, & Louie Triple-Fruit Crisp

▶◀ ▶◀ ▶◀ ▶◀ Serves 8

In honor of her triplet nephews, Daisy makes her famous crisp with a trio of tasty fruits—apples, pears, and cranberries.

Ingredients

½ cup brown sugar

⅓ cup flour

⅓ cup rolled oats

½ teaspoon cinnamon

½ teaspoon nutmeg

4 tablespoons butter, softened

3 Granny Smith apples

2 pears

¼ cup dried sweetened cranberries

¼ cup water

Directions

1. Heat the oven to 375°F.

2. In a small mixing bowl, combine the brown sugar, flour, oats, cinnamon, and nutmeg.

3. Cut the butter into eight or so pieces, and add them to the bowl. Use your fingertips to rub the butter into the sugar mixture until the topping is crumbly.

4. Core, then thinly slice the apples and pears. Layer the slices in an 8-inch-square baking pan. Top them with the dried sweetened cranberries.

5. Pour the water over the fruit. Then sprinkle on the crumb topping.

6. Bake the crisp until the fruit slices are tender, about 40 minutes. Serve it warm, either plain or topped with vanilla ice cream.

Minnie Mouse Mousse

Serves 6

Add an extra *s* to the word *mouse* and you've got another delightful Minnie-made treat—a creamy, pink strawberry mousse.

Ingredients

2 cups sliced strawberries

8 ounces whipped cream cheese

½ cup powdered sugar

1 teaspoon vanilla extract

2 cups fresh whipped cream or whipped topping

½ cup white chocolate chips

Directions

1. Combine the strawberry slices, whipped cream cheese, powdered sugar, and vanilla extract in a blender. Blend the mixture until it is smooth and creamy. Then pour it into a medium-large mixing bowl.

2. Use a rubber spatula to gently fold the whipped cream into the berry mixture.

3. When the mousse is evenly blended, spoon it into serving dishes. Chill for 2 hours or more. Top each dish with a few white chocolate chips right before serving.

Daisy's Daisy Cupcake Decorations

Makes 1 dozen

Made to order for Minnie's best friend, these celebration cupcake toppings are candy copies of Daisy's namesake flower.

Ingredients

1 dozen frosted cupcakes

White candy-coated licorice

Round yellow candy-coated chocolates

Directions

1. Lightly press a yellow candy-coated chocolate into the frosting in the middle of the cupcake top for the flower center.

2. Arrange nine or ten pieces of white candy-coated licorice around the yellow center, so that one end almost touches the yellow candy, and the other end points to the edge of the cupcake.

3. Repeat until you've decorated all the cupcakes.

Polka-dot Fruit Sundae

Makes 1

Decorated with white chocolate–filled berries, this sweet ice cream treat is proof that Minnie's got the scoop on great desserts.

Ingredients

Several fresh raspberries

Vanilla ice cream

White chocolate chips

Directions

1. Wash the raspberries with cold water. Lightly pat them dry with a paper towel.

2. Place a white chocolate chip with the tip pointing down into the hollow center of each berry.

3. Scoop some vanilla ice cream into a serving dish. Top the scoop with the berry polka dots, gently pressing them against the ice cream just until they stick in place. Enjoy!

Food styling by Edwina Stevenson

Designed by Kurt Hartman

Special thanks to
Brittany Candau, Tina DiLorenzo, Eric Geron,
and Mike, Christine, and Stella Siglain

Printed in the United States of America

First Edition
10 9 8 7 6 5 4 3 2 1

G942-9090-6-14066
Library of Congress Control Number: 2013955081
ISBN 978-1-4231-6756-3

SUSTAINABLE FORESTRY INITIATIVE — Certified Sourcing
www.sfiprogram.org
SFI-00993
This Label Applies to Text Stock Only

For more Disney Press fun, visit www.disneybooks.com